AF505961

ARLINGTON NATIONAL CEMETERY: DRAWINGS BY EWAN GIBBS

BY **RICHARD SHIFF**, WITH CONTRIBUTIONS BY EWAN GIBBS,
REBECCA A. DUNHAM, AND YASUFUMI NAKAMORI

THE MUSEUM OF FINE ARTS, HOUSTON
DISTRIBUTED BY YALE UNIVERSITY PRESS, NEW HAVEN AND LONDON

Generous funding for the exhibition
*Ewan Gibbs: Arlington National
Cemetery* and its accompanying
catalogue is provided by the
following individuals in memory
of Barry Walker:

John Blackmon and John Roberson
Jeanne and Michael Klein
Lora Reynolds and Quincy Lee
Scurlock Foundation
Lynn Goode and Harrison Williams
Amanda and Glenn Fuhrman
Lea Weingarten
Tassy and Mitch Beasley
Kelty and Rogers Crain

When I set out from England on this self-appointed mission to photograph
and then to draw the gravestones at Arlington National Cemetery, I knew
that my thoughts would be dominated by notions of loss, public service,
untimely death, and fitting memorials. What I could not have predicted was
that these very same elements would touch this project in other profound
and unforeseen ways.

I visited Arlington on May 4, 2010, and was fortunate that it
was a fine late spring day for me to take photographs. I remember feeling
surprised and moved by seeing the same level of honor accorded to the
spouses and dependent children of those who had lost their lives in service
to their country. The first grave I approached happened to be that of
a soldier's daughter who had passed away at only four days old, in 1961.

It was a life-affirming experience to spend time observing
some of the memorials of the more than three hundred thousand Americans
buried at Arlington National Cemetery, meandering slowly between the
rows of headstones, pausing to take in the gravity of the surroundings
while trying to remain focused on what I was there to do. It felt trivial
to be preoccupied with thoughts regarding the composition and framing
of images. I kept flipping back and forth, from seeing the headstones
as abstract patterns to contemplating the facts of the matter. As I have
drawn the pictures, the same dichotomy has been evident. On too many
occasions as I was engrossed in my mark-making, I would hear on the radio
some breaking news about another coalition fatality. For each report of
a British loss of life, I knew that within a week the person's body would be
flown back to within a few miles of my home, and that the cortege would
pass within a mile of my front door.

When I was living in London, it was easy to become desensi-
tized to this reality. But, having moved to a military area where some of
the parents of my children's friends are serving in the armed forces, these
losses are thankfully harder to ignore.

On leaving Arlington, I headed back to my hotel and then on to
the airport to fly to Texas for a meeting the next morning with Peter C.
Marzio, director of the Museum of Fine Arts, Houston, and Barry Walker,
curator of modern and contemporary art and of prints and drawings.

I was accompanied by Lora Reynolds, in whose gallery I exhibit my works in Austin. The meeting went better than I had dared hope, and the exhibition and this publication were set for November 2012.

Later that year, I was shocked to hear from Barry that Peter had passed away. Then, in April of this year, I learned from Lora that Barry had died unexpectedly.

Peter's and Barry's lives were cut short. Each was only sixty-seven years old, and I am sure they both had so much more to offer, as did the hundreds of thousands of people buried at Arlington, including the four-day-old baby girl, Cathleen; had she lived, she would have turned fifty last year.

Peter and Barry gave some fifty years of service between them to the MFAH. Their legacy lives on at the museum, and I have found the cooperation and support from all those with whom I had contact to be both warm and friendly, coupled with the utmost professionalism and an openness to sharing ideas and exploring possibilities.

It has been a wonderful opportunity to collaborate with the MFAH staff. I felt privileged to spend a couple of hours with Peter Marzio on that day in May 2010—to be shown around the museum by him and to see his pride in it. I was fortunate enough to spend more time with Barry Walker over the course of the last decade, benefiting from many enjoyable and educational hours in his company looking at and talking about art.

Finally, it has been a labor of love producing this body of work during the last ten months. I would like to dedicate my series of Arlington drawings to all those who rest at the cemetery, and to also dedicate this publication to the memory of Barry and Peter.

INTRODUCTION Rebecca A. Dunham

In *Ewan Gibbs: Arlington National Cemetery*, British artist Ewan Gibbs (born London, 1973) has trained his expert eye on Arlington National Cemetery to create a series of sixteen drawings based on his photographs of the historic military cemetery. These drawings depict both individual views and sweeping panoramas of the cemetery's gravestones.

Gibbs first pondered Arlington National Cemetery as a subject in late 2009. The previous year, he and his wife and two children moved to Faringdon, a sleepy market town in Oxfordshire, England. Occasionally, on his daily walks, he witnessed corteges of hearses escorting fallen soldiers from Royal Air Force Base Lyneham to the coroner's office at the John Radcliffe Hospital in Oxford. RAF Lyneham was, until its closure in 2012, the base of repatriation for British personnel killed in Afghanistan (and formerly Iraq). Faringdon, which is in between RAF Lyneham and Oxford, is also only nine miles away from RAF Brize Norton, the main air terminal for troop and supply deployments since 1944. This proximity to the reality of the sacrifices made by these young men and women was an integral motivating factor for Gibbs, who visited Arlington with the intent to make drawings of the gravestones.

At the time, Gibbs was in the midst of presenting his first solo museum exhibition at the San Francisco Museum of Modern Art, and this gave him the confidence to pursue a museum venue for the Arlington project. Gibbs enjoyed a long-standing relationship with Barry Walker, who served as curator of modern and contemporary art and also curator of prints and drawings at the Museum of Fine Arts, Houston, and who had taken an early interest in Gibbs's career. Walker and Gibbs first met in late 1999 at the artist's first international solo exhibition held at Paul Morris Gallery, New York. Gibbs felt that the Houston museum was a perfect fit for his proposed project, and Walker enthusiastically agreed. Gibbs also has a connection with Texas at large, having exhibited at Lora Reynolds Gallery in Austin on three occasions since 2005 and having traveled to Houston, Dallas, and Fort Worth.

Gibbs and Reynolds met with Walker and Peter C. Marzio, then director of the MFAH, in May 2010; shortly thereafter, the museum's Board of Trustees formally approved the project. Because photography is an integral component of Gibbs's work, he envisioned the museum displaying photographs with his drawings. Encouraged by Walker and Marzio, Gibbs consulted with Yasufumi Nakamori, associate curator of photography at the MFAH, to select photographs by artists who had inspired him in

   INTRODUCTION   Rebecca A. Dunham

his career. Together, the drawings and photographs emphasize the role our eyes play in viewing and processing visual material.

Gibbs's drawings are closely related to photography, but they do not mimic photography. Using a unique pictorial language, Gibbs re-creates photographic images in drawings that are intimate in scale. Originally, while attending Goldsmiths College at the University of London during the 1990s, he concentrated on painting interior scenes influenced by the work of Post-Impressionists and artists such as Roy Lichtenstein and fellow British painter Patrick Caulfield. "I was making paintings, and then I got in this weird position where I knew I wanted to paint but I didn't know what I wanted to paint or how, in what language. And I felt like I was being really derivative of painters I admired at the time."[1]

In 1993, Gibbs had what he calls a "eureka" moment when he happened upon a book of knitting and crochet patterns at a market stall in Brick Lane in the East End of London. He was fascinated by the book, which contained patterns of grids filled with symbols such as circles, crosses, and diagonal lines that corresponded to colored threads to be used in the production of the textiles. Gibbs decided to adopt this functional language of charts and to use it as a template for turning a found image into a drawing. In his first "knitting pattern drawing," Gibbs reinterpreted an Edward Hopper painting, which he followed with a translation of a Hopperesque photograph of a hotel interior he found in a 1960s-era holiday travel brochure.

The first element with which people engage when viewing Gibbs's drawings are the images themselves, and then they respond quickly to the pictorial language that he has employed to create them. To this day, the artist continues to follow a precise series of steps: He makes a black-and-white copy of a photograph, overlays a grid on the copy, and, working from unit to unit (bottom to top, left to right), transfers the imagery to another gridded sheet of paper by making marks that approximate the copy's tonal values. Gibbs tends to use one type of mark (circles, dots within circles, or diagonal strokes) per drawing, repeating it over and over with minute variations in pressure and thickness.

Despite the craft-based origins of Gibbs's pictorial language, it is deeply rooted in the history of art. As mentioned above, he was influenced by Post-Impressionism, but his drawings also reference Impressionism, Realism, Pointillism, Minimalism, and Pop Art. In Gibbs's book *False Starts*

(2009), the artist explains the process by way of reproducing unfinished and aborted drawings that reveal the rigid repetitiveness of mark-making. The book also underscores his objective of exploring visual perception, specifically the construction of images and how we interpret them, by de-emphasizing narrative and contextual analysis. In addition, Gibbs's technique addresses the idea of time; in today's relentlessly fast-paced society, his drawings represent a moment of reflection as the imagery appears and dissolves, dissolves and reappears.

Attempting to find the "perfect" mark, Gibbs has continually revised and refined his pictorial language. After he made his "knitting pattern drawing" that was inspired by the Hopperesque travel-brochure photograph, he continued this line of inquiry in his first body of work, Typical Interiors. While still in college, Gibbs frequented travel agencies to collect brochures, which he liked for several reasons. They contained free, ready-made images, and their content reminded him of the interiors depicted in the famous paintings he had studied in college; also, their advertising aesthetic lacked specific narratives. Noticing that each photograph was accompanied by a caption stating "typical interior," Gibbs adopted this same convention for titling his group of drawings, with individual works bearing the name of a dominant subject, such as "bed" or "desk."

Gibbs briefly flirted with color in a few of his early drawings, but he quickly abandoned it for a monochromatic scheme executed in pen and/or pencil. After cutting his source images from brochures, which he occasionally cropped, he relied on copy shops to make black-and-white copies. Digital technology and home computers and printers were not as prevalent then. In 2000, Walker acquired two "typical interiors" for the MFAH collection: *Magazine 2/7/2000 – 2/11/2000* (2000) and *Brochure 2/13/2000 – 2/17/2000* (2000). He acquired a third example in 2007: *Watch* (1997).

In his *Typical Interiors,* Gibbs strove to depict the generic environment of inexpensive hotel rooms. He hoped his blatant appropriation of advertising photographs would eliminate narrative and encourage the viewer to consider the act of looking and the construction of the drawing. But *Typical Interiors* did have inevitable undertones of a narrative, specifically feelings of isolation or loneliness. Therefore, Gibbs shifted his emphasis to the hotel facades depicted in the travel brochures, and this subject became his second body of work, Facades.

Gibbs initially created these portraits of hotels after travel-brochure images, but, in 2000, he began taking his own photographs of hotels in London and other European cities. This pursuit culminated in the 2002 publication *Facades*, which featured twenty-eight drawings based on his source photographs. At that time, Gibbs also began looking more closely at historical and contemporary photography, especially the work of Bernd and Hilla Becher, Hiroshi Sugimoto, and Eugène Atget, as well as that of canonical twentieth-century photographers such as Brassaï, Henri Cartier-Bresson, Eugene Smith, Robert Frank, Walker Evans, Berenice Abbott, and André Kertész. In terms of painters, Gibbs remained interested in artists who created paintings, drawings, and prints based on photographs. Included among this group are Vija Celmins, Chuck Close, Richard Artschwager, and Ed Ruscha.

In between taking snapshots of hotel facades, Gibbs began photographing iconic buildings, historic landmarks, street scenes and events, and generic cityscapes. To his delight, he realized his photographs were like tourists' photographs—they reflected an impartial, universal type of image. These images have become the mainstay of his practice to the present day. He refers to this body of work as Destinations, and he has made series of "destination" drawings depicting London, Paris, New York, Chicago, San Francisco, Colorado, Washington, D.C., and Austin. In 2005, Gibbs briefly returned to the use of brochure images as source material for the series of drawings of Paris.

The majority of Gibbs's *Destinations* drawings have vertical compositions and strong central motifs. Although their motifs are usually historically important, Gibbs was attracted to their iconic status because of the proliferation of photographic images portraying the motifs, which elevated them to "celebrity status." Of these works, in 2006 Walker acquired for the MFAH collection the drawing *London* (2006), which shows Tower Bridge at night.

Over the last five years, Gibbs's drawings have reflected his growing interest in other iconic U.S. subjects. Having watched several Major League Baseball games on trips to the United States, Gibbs created a group of eight drawings in 2007 depicting baseball pitchers. For this series, Gibbs gathered his source photographs from the Getty Images archive. The artist has stated: "The images I choose depict the pitchers follow-through at its most extreme. My interest is not in

the specific individuals depicted or in their celebrity status but in their
contorted forms that can only be captured and arrested by the camera.
Once chosen, I then spend days, weeks, and months translating and
celebrating each of these split seconds of extreme athleticism and
endeavor."[2] Their titles, such as *Cleveland* (2007), which Walker secured
for the MFAH, refer to the cities in which the photographs were taken,
not to the pitchers' teams.

Gibbs has also photographed and drawn fans in the bleachers
at Yankee Stadium, and his other subjects include a portrait of basketball
legend Michael Jordan and a NYPD officer in Times Square. These drawings and the ongoing *Destinations* reveal an evolution in Gibbs's pictorial
language as he willingly tackles a wider range of subjects, including land-
scapes, elements of the weather, reflective surfaces, more-animated
subjects, and moving vehicles and objects.

For the drawings in *Ewan Gibbs: Arlington National Cemetery*,
Gibbs chose to focus on America's most iconic cemetery and memorial
to war heroes. The land and buildings at Arlington National Cemetery are
deeply intertwined with American history and politics, making the site
a popular tourist and pilgrimage destination. Originally an estate owned by
the Custis-Lee family (the first U.S. President's adopted grandson, George
Washington Parke Custis, and later his daughter, Mary Anna Randolph
Custis, and her husband, General Robert E. Lee), it became a fully opera-
tional national cemetery in May 1864 in response to the overflow of Civil
War casualties near Washington, D.C.

Today, Arlington National Cemetery is the most hallowed burial
ground in the nation with more than 330,000 American servicemen and
their close family members, as well as many famous historical figures, laid
to rest on the 624-acre property. On average, the cemetery, which receives
four million visitors annually, conducts twenty-seven funeral services each
day. The impressive landscape at Arlington serves as a tribute to the service and the sacrifice of every individual buried there.

Over the course of four hours on a single day in May 2010,
Gibbs took approximately three hundred photographs while visiting
Arlington National Cemetery. He took them with a standard "tourist"
digital camera, and he used its black-and-white setting to get an immediate sense of the images as drawings, a luxury he did not have before
the advent of digital technology.

After uploading the digital images to his computer and reviewing them, Gibbs selected sixteen vertically oriented photographs to translate into drawings. He divided the series into two groups, small (sheets measuring 30.5 × 22.9 mm) and large (sheets measuring 45.7 × 30.5 mm), and their central motifs are single gravestones and sweeping panoramas of rows of gravestones, respectively. For the small drawings, Gibbs purposefully selected simple markers. For the large drawings, the repetitive rows of gravestones bear a striking formal relationship to Gibbs's pictorial language of repeated marks in orderly rows. Each of the sixteen drawings is simply titled *Arlington*.

Gibbs's regime mirrors his drawing process; the artist adheres to a strict schedule that ensures he works at his drawing board for nine to ten hours daily. When Gibbs and his family moved to Faringdon, he turned the smallest room on the third floor of their three-story, early Georgian house into a studio. Measuring ten by eight feet with a low ceiling and sloping eaves, the crammed studio contains a table topped with a tilted drawing board and piles of Faber-Castell pencils, a chair, a lamp, and shelves lined with CDs. He listens to these CDs along with live sports or podcasts of BBC radio shows while drawing. The ledges in front of the room's windows, which Gibbs blocked out to maintain even light levels throughout the day, are filled with art and travel books. Tacked and pasted to the walls are postcards, pictures his children made, future potential imagery, and his ongoing collection of the U.S. 50 State Quarters.

Tucked away in his home studio, Gibbs completed a small drawing in three to five days, while the larger ones each took up to six weeks. He typically worked on one drawing at a time. After printing copies of his photographs to scale and applying grids to them, he re-created the grids on cream-colored watercolor paper by scoring horizontal and vertical lines with a sharp tool. He recently introduced this grid-making technique, having first experimented with a round embossing tool before settling on a sewing needle. Gibbs has stated: "Although it is much more time consuming to inscribe a grid than to use printed graph paper, I made the change so as to have more control of the size of the paper, to have a heavier better quality surface, and to have a whiter ground that would give me the potential for lighter tones without the grey grid already printed on it which did not allow me to ever go really light."[3]

Rather than utilizing the entire sheets of paper, Gibbs scored and drew in their centers and left borders around the imagery. As he carefully copied his source photographs' tonal values, he did so with an "x" mark, a new mark in his repertoire. After making a few small interiors in 2010 with this mark, he concluded it is the most effective mark he has used thus far as it covers more space in the squares of his grids, thereby capturing and generating more information than other marks. In addition, the "x" marks create a secondary grid when their corners meet, making it more difficult for the viewer to focus on one square in the grid as the overall image becomes unified. Gibbs is fascinated by various readings of the "x" mark, for instance, a kiss, a multiplication sign, a capture sign in chess notation, the location of treasure on a treasure map, an incorrect answer, a signature, adult content, an unknown factor, or as the word "cross," which suggests another level of interpretation, including the importance of the cross as a Christian symbol. There is also a long tradition of creating hatching and cross-hatching marks in the history of drawing and printmaking.

In the Arlington series, Gibbs is not taking a pro- or anti-war position, but merely presenting the reality of the cemetery. The objective of his pictorial language is to explore individual visual perception. Still, the artist intends for his drawings to speak to wide audiences. His easily identifiable, iconic subjects, coupled with the intimacy of his tiny, hand-drawn marks, resonate with viewers as they consider their own personal experiences.

1. Ewan Gibbs, artist's quote, from "In the Studio," *Art + Auction* (January 2010): 40.

2. Ewan Gibbs, artist's quote, from press release for exhibition *Ewan Gibbs: Pictures of Pitchers*, Lora Reynolds Gallery, March 8 – April 19, 2008.

3. Ewan Gibbs, email to Barry Walker, April 16, 2012.

DOUBLE-BLUR Richard Shiff

Reality is a perceptual blur. Or forever "out of focus," as Ewan Gibbs would prefer to regard it. We never know the precise relationship of what we see to what exists, or between our visual memory and its technical codes of translation. "In some of my drawings I use a hard line that can describe blur or movement, and in others I may describe a hard edge with a soft mark," Gibbs states. His clear, fixed line can represent an unstable condition, and a soft touch can represent hardness. He adds: "Is [a] Seurat painting in or out of focus?"[1] The fine screen of colored dots in a work by Georges Seurat might enhance resolution or just as readily pixelate the image. Perhaps the attitude that a viewer brings to such a picture determines what its technique accomplishes—for this individual, at this moment, given the interpretive method applied. There are many conditional factors. Why would any viewer be certain of his or her specific perceptual judgment?

      The failure to see clearly—or, more to the point, to evaluate unambiguously the significance for reality of what we do see—is not our failing alone. Ironically, this lapse is a feature of the world we observe, as if the world were designed to evade our attempts at representing it.

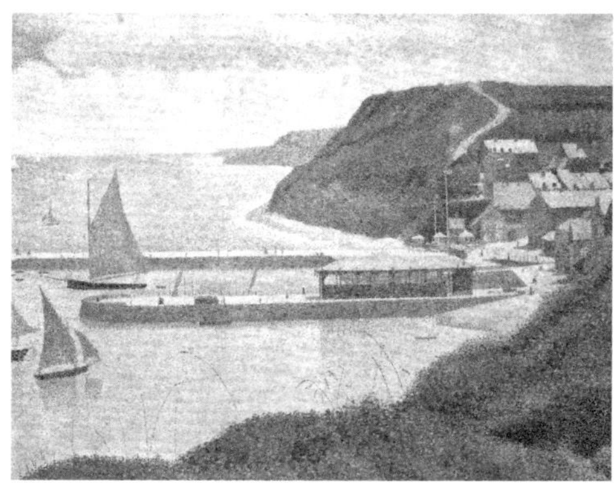

Georges Seurat, 1859–1891, *Port-en-Bessin, avant-port, marée haute* (*Harbor at Port-en-Bessin at High Tide*), 1888, oil on canvas, 26.4 × 32.3 in. (67 × 82 cm), Musée d'Orsay, Paris, France. Photo: Hervé Lewandowski © RMN-Grand Palais / Art Resource, NY

Every accurate representation falls into imprecision, even for those—no, *particularly* for those—who are most sophisticated at controlling a representational medium, whether visual, aural, or verbal. Experienced artists understand the failure of representation even as they create convincing descriptions, depictions, symbols, and images. John Ruskin argued this point in his multi-volume *Modern Painters*, in a section dated 1856. Making his case, he marshaled a typographical rhetoric of italics and all caps, a style that may seem at once overbearing and quaint. His message nevertheless remains "modern"—timely for us today: "There is a continual mystery caused throughout *all* spaces, caused by the absolute infinity of things. WE NEVER SEE ANYTHING CLEARLY.... Under what a universal law of obscurity we live ... [N]othing can be right, till it is unintelligible."[2] Perhaps Ruskin chose to shout his uppercase realization because he knew it would strike others as counterintuitive. It does still. Do we not see clearly enough already? After all, the human race is surviving.

Invoking mystery, infinitude, and obscurity, Ruskin's statement is itself mystifying. But the enduring boldness and paradoxical clarity of his thoughts about the ultimate imprecision of vision has impressed Gibbs, who in February 2012 began reading Ruskin and taking notes. He encountered Ruskin's reference to unintelligibility not in its original source but in the context of a like-minded publication of 1857, *The Elements of Drawing*, where the passage appeared quoted in a scholarly introduction to a modern edition.[3] Gibbs marked the passage in the margin of his copy of the book. Precision in seeing is central to his web of aesthetic concerns, as it was to Ruskin's. He is not seeking a preferential way for things to look (a "true" vision), but investigating *how* vision operates, how things may look under various conditions of viewing and representing. His probe into visual perception takes a number of quirky turns, fascinating to the outside observer, and more unusual than Gibbs himself may realize. Of course, what he does appears entirely logical, perhaps even obvious, to *him*, dictated by his interests and an outgrowth of the continuing evolution of his perceptual experience. People shape their experience to suit their needs; perception involves feedback.

Gibbs photographs subjects that appeal to him for one reason or another, usually multiple reasons. His photography may suit a strategic purpose in furthering a theme in his art, such as investigating a tourist's sense of the American experience (Gibbs is British but more traveled in the

United States than most Americans). It may also satisfy a half-conscious emotional need. Between 2010 and 2012, Arlington National Cemetery in northern Virginia, just outside Washington, became a focus of Gibbs's attention. In his preface to this catalogue, he refers to absorbing the "gravity of the surroundings" at Arlington while nevertheless responding to the "abstract patterns of the rows of graves." This type of divided attention is typical of him: he is simultaneously the wide-eyed, impressionable observer of a socially and politically charged environment and the canny artist assessing the potential for image-making. The artist is not always the emotional individual, and the emotional individual is not always the artist; yet Gibbs's arresting, haunting series of images of Arlington is a product of the combination.

 Gibbs has acknowledged his special sensitivity to the reality of death and its rituals: "I think about death many more times a day than most of my friends and family." He renders views of Arlington objectively, but the location has a subjective appeal beyond his cultivated interest in the historical meaning it holds for Americans, along with other national monuments. Part of the emotional draw of this site relates to the proximity of Gibbs's Oxfordshire home to a British air base that receives the dead from the ongoing war in Afghanistan. Gibbs often contemplates this manifestation of death and feels surrounded by it, even though he and his family have not been directly affected.

 Under different circumstances, Gibbs has observed the traces of death in Oxfordshire and in Arlington. Like his photographs, he is a witness. How good a witness? He remarks on the irony that although all photography has a blur or resolution problem built into it, we continue to refer to a "photographic" memory as supremely detailed. It is as if people would profit from converting human perception to the mechanical condition of photography, for they would become better witnesses. When Gibbs translates his photographic images of Arlington into drawings, he transfers the vision of one medium into that of another with as much rigor as he can muster, yet without assuming that photography has the upper hand. If he wanted to stress fidelity to his source, he might simply project the photographic image directly onto the surface of his white sheets of paper. Many artists, including those comfortable with the designation "photorealist," have worked by various means of indexical tracing or physical transfer (for example, using solvents to imprint images onto paper as a base for pictorial elaboration). Curiously, such a direct process of conversion by contact is too direct for Gibbs. It would short-circuit the factor of visual experience that most concerns him — the temporality of vision.

Gibbs's process attends to two types of temporal gap, each introducing either better focus or more blur, depending on how we spin the analysis. First, there is the time differential between Gibbs's activity in Arlington as a tourist-photographer and his work in his Oxfordshire studio, drawing what he has photographed. Does his response to the imagery change in the interval? At the very least, it is affected by the accumulation of images around a theme, just as one's attitude toward a particular aspect of life may be altered by additional experience. Both at the site and in the studio, Gibbs became increasingly sensitive to the effect of areas of hilly cemetery ground on thoughts of the ubiquity and magnitude of death. In Arlington, the benign traces of death — the gravestones, death's cultural signs — appear to pass over all contours of the land, unimpeded. In the sixth large drawing in the series, an illuminated, diagonally oriented spread of grass, in concert with a rise and then a drop in elevation, creates a break between the limited number of graves in the foreground and what appears as an infinite array in the background. In retrospect, the play between the particularity of a limited number of graves and the generality of an unlimited number generates a complex set of thoughts about life, death, history, and memory. The philosophical and poetic potential of such an image is boundless. Gibbs's vision, fixed in a photograph and slowly reconstituted in a drawing, acts on his thinking over time. The temporality of his artistic process might result in an intense concentration on a single aspect of his theme or, to the contrary, expand his thinking and overwhelm his feelings, even to the point of distraction.

To some degree, all images are philosophically, poetically, and emotionally evocative; and perhaps all artists deal with the implications. The second type of temporal gap that concerns Gibbs is, however, peculiar and raises issues less familiar — the gap between *looking* at a detail within a photograph, just a bit of something, and *making* this a detail of a drawing. This temporal delay, no matter how slight, occurs within the representational process itself. It may be the very space of creativity. Or it may be an impediment to the execution of the creative act. The difficulties of Gibbs's studio operation — its intensive labor, eye to hand to eye — are analogous to what a nineteenth-century artist, using a live model in an atelier, would encounter. Gibbs's more traditional counterpart would inspect the turn of an elbow or a hip, looking first to the model, then to the paper, then back to the model to make a judgment. Now a photograph is the model, and it becomes as thoroughly alive as a vivid memory under the conditions set by Gibbs's drawing. He retells the photographic story as a process of observation, a slow-motion account of what otherwise may pass too quickly.[4] He measures the time of an individual drawing in weeks, not days. The extent of his examination of the convergence of photography and drawing, this blurring of the two mediums, is unexpected.

We may recognize that Gibbs's efforts enhance the understanding of perception, but how they do so may seem obscure. His drawings uncover problems we did not know we had. Gibbs realizes that if his representational process is to succeed, the translation must be "close" not only in a conceptual sense but also physically. He takes his sense of closeness to a physical limit without imagining that he can ever avoid some degree of failure, the factor of lapse embodied in the temporal gap, which is also a spatial gap. Two visions of a situation separated by a glance or a blink cannot coincide. Gibbs acts out the conditions of perceptual failure as a way to understand them. More than a witness, he is a witness to witnessing.[5]

In *The Elements of Drawing*, Ruskin concluded: "Good drawing is … an *abstract* of natural facts: you cannot represent all that you would, but must continually be falling short, whether you will or no, of the force, or quantity, of Nature."[6] An abstract is reductive; it may capture a desirable essence but fails the model by lacking specific aspects of it. If all representations fall short, and if denial of this experiential reality would be fantasy, then how does one set about to fall *less* short? This is the pragmatic question Gibbs asks. He suggests that his photograph and his emergent drawing must be brought into the closest proximity, virtually touching, though not. He makes no pretense that the representation avoids introducing sources of blur to the body of evidence or information. His method admits a certain degree of defeat from the start, a result of even the slightest temporal gap. To focus on this *minimum* degree of blur is the aim of Gibbs's empirical aesthetics: "It is not possible to look at the [photographic] source at the same time as making the [drawing] mark. I get them as close to each other as possible to limit the time my mind must retain the information." Because the photograph and the drawing are of the same subject—one imitates, but does not explicitly interpret, the other—they count as conceptually proximate. With a logic so direct that it seems either ingenious or foolish, Gibbs reasons that reducing the physical distance from one target of his gaze to the other — from source image to drawing-in-progress — reduces the chance that his mind, and so his eye, wanders from precision in both memory and rendering. If the conceptual play of memory has no opportunity to spring into action, simple visual memory has a chance to work in peace, perhaps to activate hidden potential. Physical proximity becomes an aid to stabilizing the conceptual likeness, leaving vision to do nothing but see. Put another way: Gibbs worries that his visual thought will fall victim to distraction if his gaze turns too slowly from his photograph to his drawing. When precision is at issue, milliseconds count.

Objects can never be close enough. Eye and hand are never fast enough. The seventh large-format drawing of the Arlington series, shown while still in progress, reveals that Gibbs printed the digital photographic source on graph paper to facilitate transferring values of gray from the photographic grid to the corresponding drawing grid. With each unit of the drawing measuring 3 mm by 3 mm within a total area of 360 mm by 270 mm, the number of units is 10,800 (a relatively modest figure within the range with which Gibbs has worked). Each of these units contains a single

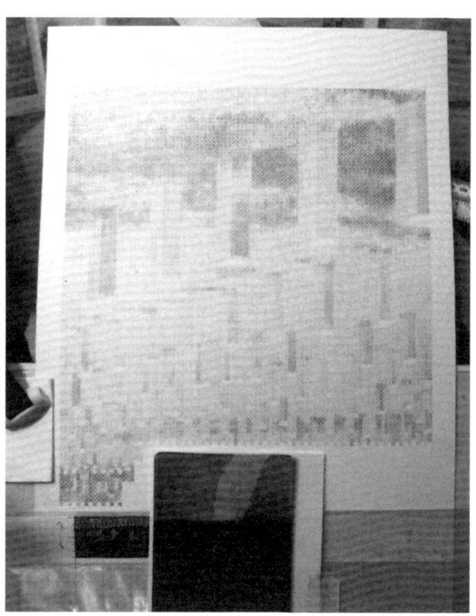

Ewan Gibbs, British, born 1973, Drawing, in process, for the Arlington series, 2012, Courtesy of the artist.

freehand mark, an *x* that extends from corner to corner, crossing its diagonals at the center and ending at the scored, colorless lines of the grid. Gibbs wants to avoid being affected by recognition of the representational content as he draws, so he views only the immediate area to be transferred, bringing it into the focus of proximity by folding all other segments of the photograph underneath the leading edge, out of sight (on page 25, the small, exposed area of the photograph is at the lower left). To reduce the play of recognition still further, he works with the image inverted: "By drawing upside-down, I am deliberately trying not to think."

In his early gridded drawings, those completed before 2000, Gibbs determined the specific character of his chosen graphic mark—its thinness or thickness, its lightness or darkness—by averaging the tonal qualities of the corresponding unit of the source photograph. This is a common procedure among artists who work with gridded arrays of hand-rendered picture elements. Gibbs noticed that drawings made in this manner generate pixelation, a type of blur, just as video and computer images do. When pixelation occurs, it forces the viewer to turn from seeing the image to attending to its electronic or material constitution. Gibbs developed a strange way to alter this effect—strange because it either escapes notice, or when noticed, does not register as interference within the system. Becoming aware of what Gibbs has done is rather like detecting a material gap full of visual information, as opposed to a gap as empty as the word normally implies.

What replaces averaging within the grid units? When Gibbs draws the *x* (or any other repeating mark), one to a grid unit, he imitates or captures only those tonal values that correspond to the precise location of this form, this *x*; it is as if the *x* were an adhesive traced over the photographic source, lifted, and dropped into the drawing.[7] The actual graphic configuration of the chosen mark determines which tonal values of the photographic source will reappear within the drawing and which will not. The form of an *x* is full at its center where its diagonals cross and empty in the four right triangles that extend to the sides of the (usually) square grid unit that contains this figure. Among other curious possibilities, the *x*-form dictates that a bit of darkness in the photograph may become pure whiteness in the drawing—blank paper. Here is an analogy: if Gibbs's drawing paper were photo-sensitive, he would be disabling some of the photo-sensors on its surface, leaving only those that together constituted the shape of an *x*. More to the point, his *x* eliminates the potential of certain areas of the drawing paper to receive a deposit of graphite. "My drawings are full of consistent gaps in information over the field of the image," he explains. Sometimes the gaps affect legibility, but often do not. In either case, we see or sense a difference—a gap, a blur—even if we are hard put to articulate its significance. Cognizant of what happens in a drawing, Gibbs evokes a parallel in ordinary perception: "As we walk around, we can see many things but do not look at them." A vision of things registers; but, without being assigned conceptual significance, it stimulates no analysis. Things merely appear.

"If they fall within the x," Gibbs states, "they make it into the drawing." "They" refers to the features (the "many things") of the representational photograph. The result of Gibbs's unusually chancy process is more readily visible in some features than in others. Note how his drawings represent the individual blades of grass that stand in front of the light, nearly uniform surfaces of the Arlington gravestones. In the fourth and the seventh small-format drawings, the grass seems to granulate rather than pixelate, if this distinction has merit. Inspection shows bits of graphite "grass" here and there, with segments seemingly missing (the gravestone lettering appears and disappears similarly). Despite the gaps, the illusion of stalks of grass seems complete from a distance. Gibbs's photographic print is itself a digital image, which means that it too must have gaps, a limited resolution. But its inherent electronic grid—not the relatively coarse grid the artist imposes on it for the purpose of transference—is much finer than the grid of the drawing. By comparison, the photograph appears analog, continuous, all parts present. Gibbs imitates this analog appearance by treating each digital x in his drawing as if it were an analog trace of the corresponding location in the photograph. The image, however discontinuous, assumes an organic quality rather than a mechanical one, even within the gridded context. Pictorial description of remarkable delicacy is the result.

Despite competing theories of the ultimate constitution of the natural world—ubiquitous waves, subatomic particles, quantum levels— to human perception, things appear analog. Natural vision does not see nature otherwise, even though our representational systems do. When the sun sets, the reddish colors near the horizon transform into bluish colors above, without noticeable division of the innumerable intermediate hues. In various technical senses, each of our many representational media, even

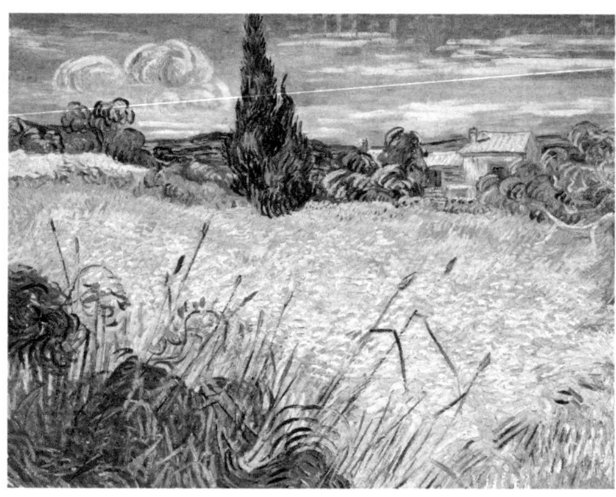

Vincent van Gogh, Dutch, 1853–1890, *Landscape with Green Corn*, 1889, oil on canvas, 27.9 × 35. 8 in. (71 × 91 cm), Narodni Galerie, Prague, Czech Republic. Photo courtesy Narodni Galerie, Prague, Czech Republic/The Bridgeman Art Library

conventional analog photography, is a digital process. Each medium has its resolution limit, where the analog effect reduces to constituent fragments of material substance. The analog digitizes, although not in an engineer's sense of this concept.[8]

When Gibbs invoked the example of Seurat, he was considering how the painter had rendered the long strands of grass in the foreground of one of his views of Port-en-Bessin. "Is the Seurat painting in or out of focus?" he asked. Because the tall grasses are so slight and Seurat's repetitive mark has its own pragmatic scale (responding to the character of his brushes, the viscosity of his paint, and other material factors), it could extend thinness or smallness only so far. Seurat resorted to leaving spaces between the individual dots that trace the grasses, as if to "thin" their average effect. Had he placed two dots beside each other, the grasses would thicken unreasonably. So a spatial gap appears that signifies something other than a break in the represented object; and if noticed, it directs attention from Seurat's seaside theme to his aesthetic fabrication. Seurat's contemporary, Vincent van Gogh, represented grasses and other delicately formed vegetation in a different way, using a few foreground elements to describe the organic structure schematically, then mobilizing an abstract system of marks to convey the presence of the same or similar vegetation as a mass or multiple. If Seurat's art has a base in regularity and uniformity, Van Gogh's, by comparison, is an irregular composite. Yet both painters made so many ad hoc decisions, that these characterizations blur the reality. For the same reason, we should hesitate to characterize Gibbs. To make an *x* that paradoxically marks lightness rather than darkness, he could, of course, draw the two diagonals as thinly and lightly as possible. But in certain drawings — the fourth large-format Arlington study is an example — he chose a different path. He outlined the *x*. This eliminates the problem of a visual accent appearing where the diagonals of the *x* cross. "When viewing the drawing from a couple of feet away, you cannot see how the marks are made," Gibbs states: "You just see the light tone."

We see and represent within shifting limits. Ruskin gave an example: if we inspect paper closely, we can detect the threads that form it, yet we still fail to observe "the fine fibers which shoot off from every thread."[9] His shorthand for this condition of perceptual inadequacy was "the absolute infinity of things."[10] The desire to see more, as a path to understanding more of the totality, cannot be met simply by moving closer. We will never comprehend the infinity. Focusing on one detail merely blurs another. When Paul Cézanne painted the portrait of a writer, he depicted the subject at his desk with several open books before him and numerous

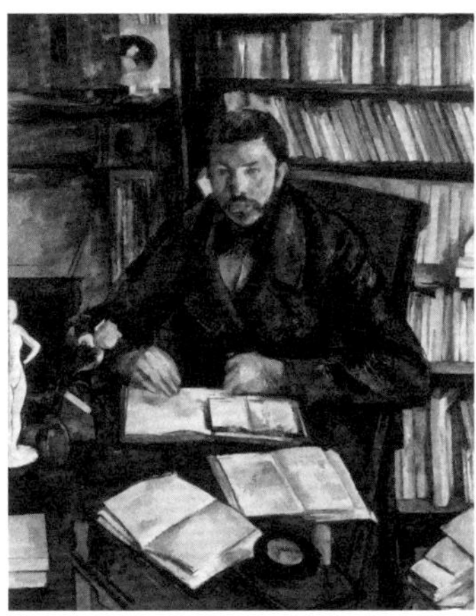

Paul Cézanne, French, 1839–1906, *Gustave Geffroy*, 1895–96, oil on canvas, 46 × 35.2 in. (117 × 89.5 cm), Musée d'Orsay, Paris, France. Photo: Gianni Dagli Orti / The Art Archive at Art Resource, NY

shelved books behind. Rather than break the rhythm of component strokes or adjust the implied degree of focus, Cézanne chose to ignore the print on the open pages and the lettering on the spines of the bindings.[11] We can fantasize that Cézanne intuited one of Ruskin's lessons: "draw [the spines of books] simply as they appear, giving the perfect look of neat lettering; which, nevertheless, must be absolutely illegible."[12] Cézanne's blank pages and bindings represent illegibility in the extreme, yet we have no difficulty interpreting what we see in the picture. Illegibility represents the reality of a shifting focus. The principle might even hold—Gibbs implies that it does—for the gap between looking and rendering. If so, any act of representation that requires both elements cannot fully succeed. Looking interferes with rendering; rendering interferes with looking.

This conclusion may push both Ruskin and Gibbs too far. But many of Ruskin's problematic examples sounded an experiential chord in Gibbs, as if the artist had already absorbed the same experiential truths, along with all their ironies, while seeking his own successes. What would constitute success in drawing? Success comes when the points of perceptual failure in representation instruct the artist and, beyond this, develop a potential to instruct others—about the nature of vision.

In 2009, a few years before Gibbs discovered his affinity to Ruskin, he published an extensive selection of his representational drawings that, for one reason or another, had gone astray. He called these incomplete images "false starts."[13] Rather than correct them, he decided he must abandon them; in his estimation, they were irredeemable. We might wonder why a drawing could not be corrected in some way, to avoid complete loss of the invested effort. But Gibbs works in terms of systems of equivalences, and despite the fact that his technique generates surprises as he executes it, his method is unforgiving. He chooses a certain graphic mark (a slash or a circle, for example, or the *x* of the Arlington series), and, as we know, applies this same mark repeatedly to articulate a fine grid. Gibbs abandons a drawing of this type if he perceives that the system is leading him away from the reality of the source. This undesirable tendency is likely to be cumulative. For instance, if Gibbs were to begin with an area of relative lightness, he might realize at some point that this tonal area was already too dark to allow him to darken other areas of the grid proportionately, passing into the darkest areas of the source image with appropriate gradation. From previous experience, he would recognize when

a particular drawing might be heading off a cliff, were he to remain true
to his system of rendering. He would know by eye, hand, and his practice
of drawing (not by any theoretical formulation) how the failure would look,
and nothing of value would come from pursuing *this* drawing further. Yet
any point of failure might be instructive to others. Taken as clear examples
of how a rational representational method can distort what it aims to represent, Gibbs's "false starts" are like a first lesson in unintelligibility.
Beyond this primer of declared failures, unintelligibility also arises from
representations we incline to regard as successful.

Gibbs read Ruskin's statement on unintelligibility just as he
was reaching the final stage of his Arlington project, producing the actual
exhibition drawings. This is coincidence; Ruskin had no direct influence
on the course of Gibbs's studio work. But through Ruskin, he discovered
that his own representational issues and even some of his remedies had
previously been explored in a nineteenth-century context. Ruskin and
Gibbs share the problems associated with the look of lettered inscriptions,
rendered indistinct by distance, and the look of grass, inherently indistinct because the individual elements become lost in the mass. In a single
statement (already quoted in some of its parts), Ruskin alluded to the
difficulties of lettering and grass, perhaps because he was choosing problems that any student of drawing would be able to discover in his or her
own domestic environment: "Try to draw the books accurately [from a dis-
tance], with the titles of the backs and patterns on the bindings as you
see them.... You are... to draw them simply as they appear, giving the perfect look of neat lettering; which, nevertheless, must be absolutely illegible.... Try to draw a bank of grass... and you will soon begin to understand
under what a universal law of obscurity we live.... [N]othing can be right,
till it is unintelligible."[14] Gibbs marked this passage as well as one he
encountered somewhat later: "There is no general way of doing *any* thing;
no recipe can be given you for so much as the drawing of a cluster of
grass.... [L]ook at it and try to draw it as it is."[15]

In drawing from a source, and in the representational process
in general, the lived image is a rumor as much as it is a blur. It passes
from one projective state to another; each has intelligibility, yet each also
lacks intelligibility. Rumors need to be tested, that is, verified; and so it
is with images. When the source is a photograph, it already projects a situation of depth onto a planar surface, just as a drawing does. But even

when the source is ordinary vision, as when a traditional studio artist uses a live model, projection is involved. The physical perspective of the artist, the socio-cultural perspective, the emotional perspective, the specific artist's interests and sensitivities at the particular moment—each of these factors bends the image away from whatever normative axis a theory of vision assigns to it. There are too many variables to allow successful generalization. Yet representations do nothing if not generalize. They generalize by establishing an identity or type. Identity is a trap for the image, constricting its open potential for meaning.

Projections share the resolution problem—if they focus here, they fail to focus there. Rumors exaggerate this, neglect that. In Gibbs's views of Arlington, the pictorial rumor passes from a photograph organized by optics and electronics to a drawing organized by eye and hand. How different are the two projections, and in what respect might the differences matter? Gibbs's x-configuration inserts an interpretive filter between the photographic source and the graphic target. As common as Gibbs's filter-marks are—the slash or slant, the circle, the x—they fail to maintain neutrality. His filters introduce semiotic, cultural connotations and the kind of thinking that his upside-down technique strains to eliminate. We call an x a cross, he notes, and this suggests "the Christian symbol associated with the cemetery." We never escape the extent of our culture. For Gibbs, and most likely for the rest of us, an x or cross is also "a kiss, a multiplication sign, to capture in chess notation, the X on a treasure map . . . X as a legally acceptable signature . . . X-rated."

Gibbs has used grids to structure his renderings throughout his mature artistic career. Is a grid neutral? Perhaps in theory, not in practice. When the model is Arlington, the subject has already been gridded. The rows of gravestones extend over land of varied elevation, with which the geometric order moves in tandem. Gibbs is intrigued by the thought that his grid of x's can be applied to a cemetery grid. These two grids are incommensurable, yet one takes the measure of the other. Gibbs wagers that a grid of x's can succeed at representing his experience at and of Arlington. He dares not claim that his x's make the experience of Arlington intelligible.

To paraphrase Ruskin's statement: being right about nature and our natural vision of it entails becoming unintelligible. In representation, we experience the unintelligible. Yet we continue to photograph, to draw, to paint. As part of the same statement, Ruskin concluded that attempts at representation allow us to "perceive that all *distinct* drawing must be *bad* drawing" (his emphasis).[16] As he attempted to render pine trees on a distant slope, four miles off, Ruskin observed the tension between two sets of limits—those of his vision and those of his medium. Call this play between eye and matter *double-blur.* Ruskin's vision was as natural as the pines at which he directed it. But his material medium also had its particular nature, not to be abused. The pines, Ruskin noted, "were not mere dots of color which I saw on the hill, but something full of essence of pine … assuredly they were more than dots of color. And yet not one of their boughs or outlines could be distinctly made out, or distinctly drawn. Therefore, if I had drawn either a definite pine, or a dot, I should have been equally wrong, the right lying in an inexplicable, almost inimitable, confusion between the two."[17]

To illustrate a pine with its characteristic branching and foliage would be to depict what Ruskin never actually saw, at least not on the occasion in question. Perhaps he knew from the geography of the site that the distant objects must be trees, and that the trees must be pines. But the objects he discerned did not appear the way pines appear when drawn definitively *as pines.* Ruskin had a lesson to teach—how to draw or paint "what you *see*" as opposed to "what you *know*"— two different senses of rightness.[18] We know pines. We see … what? Dots? Dots like Seurat's? Dots like Gibbs's bits of grass or lettering that happen to lie in the path of an *x*? For Ruskin, to draw a dot instead of a pine-form was to choose one of two extremes, converting organic representation to formal abstraction. Neither extreme—stock illustration (the pine), arbitrary design (the dot)—would prove emotionally satisfying. Ruskin's solution to the problem of drawing was to leave "confusion between the two."

Without having read Ruskin until 2012, Gibbs seems to have practiced Ruskin's technique of double-blur both before and while creating his drawings for the Arlington series. "Nothing can be right"—in perception—"till it is unintelligible." Perception loses intelligibility because it is part nature and part sign. A mere mark is the surrogate for nature's complexity. How much can a mark indicate? "What we call seeing a thing clearly," Ruskin argued, "is only seeing enough of it to *make out what it is.*" Every painting and drawing, every coded system of representation, risks defining its model too precisely. Beyond the minimum "point of intelligibility," the temptation is to develop the terms that a definition dictates, once the concept or identity of the model has taken hold.[19] An object defined as a pine will be rendered more pine-like than it appears. Groping toward intelligibility, a representation faces an unexpected hazard—false intelligibility, a deceptive consistency that masks actual contradictions. Any convincing characterization is a species of blur. Curves bend straight lines in their direction, extending the motif where it is not. Straight lines take the bend out of curves. One way or another, an accomplished representation does its object injustice; yet such injustice is "true" to the insecure status of human perception.

Ruskin concluded that the inescapable loss of intelligibility is "right." Is death unintelligible? If so, the thematic model for Gibbs's Arlington series corresponds to the lesson of his visual investigation. The artist's intelligence shines through this lesson, despite the obscurity of death and the double-blur of its pictorial perception.

1. The quoted statements and the epigraph are from Ewan Gibbs, email to the author, July 17, 2012. All subsequent quotations attributed to Gibbs are from his conversations with the author between January 2012 and July 2012, either in person or by email. In exchanges over several years, Gibbs has generously shared his thoughts, which are the foundation of this commentary. I thank Jason A. Goldstein for aid in research.

2. John Ruskin, *Modern Painters*, 5 vols. (London: J. M. Dent, 1906 [1843–1860]), 4:55, 58.

3. John Ruskin, *The Elements of Drawing* (New York: Dover, 1971 [1857]), x. Lawrence Campbell authored the introduction. Gibbs inscribed his copy of the book, indicating that he began reading it on February 23, 2012.

4. Ruskin recommended learning from the use of photographs as models, along with works by master artists. The instructive advantage of photography was its naive capture of subtle gradations of tone in nature. See Ruskin, *The Elements of Drawing*, 59–60, 100–101.

5. Gibbs's concerns recall those of C. S. Peirce: "Every lawyer knows how difficult it is for witnesses to distinguish between what they have seen and what they have inferred.…A percept.…does not describe itself"; Charles Sanders Peirce, "Questions Concerning Certain Faculties Claimed for Man" (1868), "Telepathy" (1903), *Collected Papers*, eds. Charles Hartshorne, Paul Weiss, and Arthur W. Burks, 8 vols. (Cambridge, MA: Harvard University Press, 1958–1960), 5:138, 7:372.

6. Ruskin, *The Elements of Drawing*, 200 (original emphasis).

7. I asked Gibbs whether he was aware of any other artist who works in this manner, as opposed to using a method of averaging. He knows of no other, nor do I.

8. See Richard Shiff, "Realism of Low Resolution: Digitisation and Modern Painting," in Terry Smith, ed., *Impossible Presence: Surface and Screen in the Photogenic Era* (Chicago: University of Chicago Press, 2001), 124–56.

9. Ruskin, *Modern Painters*, 4:56.

10. Ruskin, *Modern Painters*, 4:55.

11. Cézanne introduced a fragment of large print—"… SOIR"?—at the upper left margin of the painting. It may be part of the title of an illustrated magazine, but this is only a perceptual surmise.

12. Ruskin, *Modern Painters*, 4:57. Cézanne probably never read Ruskin, but his writings were admired by other French artists of the time. Paul Signac quoted a passage from Ruskin's *The Elements of Drawing* (147), regarding the importance of gradual variation in color and line; see Paul Signac, *D'Eugène Delacroix au néo-impressionnisme*, ed. Françoise Cachin (Paris: Hermann, 1978 [1899]), 132–33.

13. Ewan Gibbs, *False Starts* (Faringdon: Folly Books, 2009).

14. Ruskin, *Modern Painters*, 4:57–58; *The Elements of Drawing*, ix–x.

15. Ruskin, *The Elements of Drawing*, 97 (original emphasis).

16. Ruskin, *Modern Painters*, 4:58.

17. Ruskin, *Modern Painters*, 4:57.

18. Ruskin, *Modern Painters*, 4:57 (original emphasis).

19. Ruskin, *Modern Painters*, 4:55 (original emphasis).

BETWEEN PHOTOGRAPHY AND MEMORY: EWAN GIBBS'S DRAWINGS OF ARLINGTON NATIONAL CEMETERY

Yasufumi Nakamori

To induce the full, sensorial experience of involuntary memory, a photograph
must be transformed. Something must be done to the photograph to pull it
(and us) out of the past into the present.

— Geoffrey Batchen, *Forget Me Not: Photography and Remembrance*, 2004

In this brief essay, I will discuss my thoughts on seeing Ewan Gibbs's recent
drawings of the gravestones at Arlington National Cemetery in relation
to his own photographs of the same, reflecting on the transformation from
these photographs to the graphite drawings and considering some of the
ways in which they explore the issue of memory. In this deliberate transformation process, Gibbs dilutes the presence of a monument, ultimately
dissolving the gravestone into an ephemeral shadow. He deconstructs and
alchemizes the source photographic image with a pencil on watercolor
paper using his signature system of mark-making. In addition to discussing
the connections between Gibbs's photographs and drawings, I will propose
comparisons between Gibbs's drawings and two photographs by William
Henry Fox Talbot (1800–1877): *The Nelson Column in Trafalgar Square under
Construction* [*The Base of the column, before the addition of Landseer's
Lions*] (1844) and *The Tomb of Sir Walter Scott* (c. 1844).[1]

These two images are among the approximately forty photographs that
Gibbs personally selected from the collections of the Museum of Fine Arts,
Houston (MFAH), to be shown together with his Arlington drawings in the
exhibition *Ewan Gibbs: Arlington National Cemetery* (MFAH, November 11,
2012–February 10, 2013). Although separated by more than a century,
Gibbs's drawings and Talbot's mid-nineteenth-century salted paper prints
are linked in several ways: the two British artists deal with the issues
of memory and the monument, and their works involve the translation of
a photographic image into something ephemeral that transcends time
and has lasting import.

ARLINGTON NATIONAL CEMETERY: FROM PHOTOGRAPH TO DRAWING

Gibbs's sixteen graphite drawings that are reproduced in this
book portray a selection of gravestones at Arlington National Cemetery.
Gibbs's drawings were based on his own digital photographs shot during
a single day at the site; Gibbs then by hand transferred the photos to a

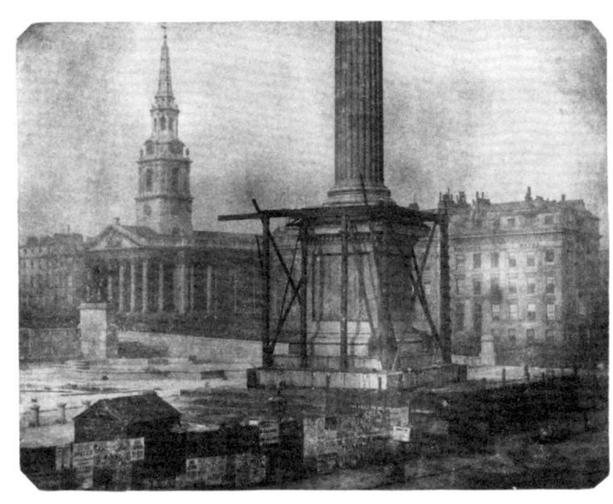

William Henry Fox Talbot, British, 1800–1877, *The Nelson Column in Trafalgar Square under Construction* [*The Base of the column, before the addition of Landseer's Lions*], 1844, salted paper print, 6 $^{11}/_{16}$ × 8 $^{5}/_{16}$ in. (17 × 21.1 cm), the Museum of Fine Arts, Houston, museum purchase with funds provided by the Brown Foundation Accessions Endowment Fund, The Manfred Heiting Collection, 2004.691.

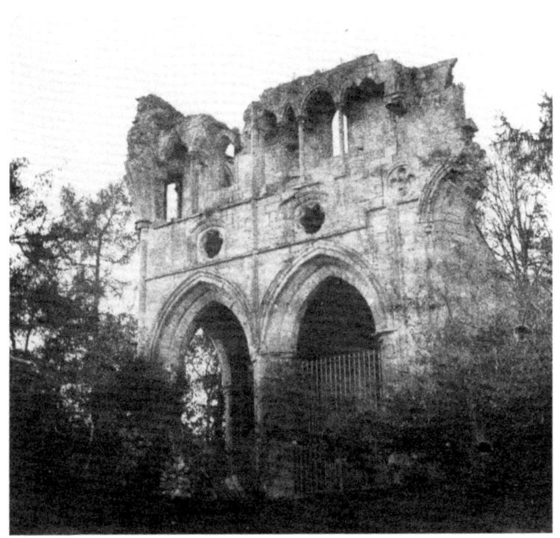

William Henry Fox Talbot, British, 1800–1877, *The Tomb of Sir Walter Scott*, c. 1844, salted paper print, 7 $^{5}/_{16}$ × 8 $^{13}/_{16}$ in. (18.6 × 22.4 cm), the Museum of Fine Arts, Houston, gift of the Lynch Foundation, courtesy of Mrs. Efrem Kurtz in honor of David Warren, 94.615.

manually gridded watercolor paper using his unique notational system that applies an x-shaped mark in either a 1-, 2-, 3-, 4-, or 5-mm grid. In this very labor-intensive process, he controls not only the size of the mark, but also its density, using a B-grade pencil. (Please see the essay by Richard Shiff in this book for a detailed discussion of Gibbs's drawing technique.) Gibbs's drawings are complex and nuanced; they go beyond mere representations of his own documentation, as they are charged not only with the unavoidable implications of the serious subject matter but also with metamorphosing a monument (that by its nature is permanent) into something fleeting, evaporating, fragmented, and abstract, yet still symbolic of endurance. As a result, his images hover like ghosts between representations and memories.

Gibbs lives in Faringdon, in Oxfordshire, England, not far from Wootton Bassett, a town known for its role as a repatriation point for the bodies of fallen British soldiers. Gibbs, like many of his neighbors in Wootton Bassett and in its surrounding areas, were witnesses to corteges that would pass through the area en route to returning the bodies of soldiers lost in recent wars in the Middle East to their families. Having previously focused on vernacular and historically significant sites (from anonymous hotel facades and interiors in Europe, to historical statues and the architecture of Austin, Texas, such as a Texas Ranger statue in front of the State Capital Building), he developed an interest in rendering an iconic site that represents military fatalities, without asserting a specific political view or romanticizing or heroicizing the casualties of war. Historically, images of the Arlington gravestones have been seen widely as signifiers of the heroism of the fallen soldiers. Viewing such images in films, photographs, or even on the Internet is a fairly familiar, global contemporary experience. Gibbs's decision to create drawings of the American national monument/ memorial derives from his continuing interest in drawing recognizable landmarks, as seen in his previous works about architecture and public spaces, most notably, in London and New York. In the United States, where he began showing his work in 1999, Gibbs operates as a foreigner who adopts a neutral position as a *flâneur*, walking around, snapping pictures, and observing people, all the while maintaining a little distance from his subjects.

To begin his work on the Arlington drawing series, in May 2010, Gibbs visited the cemetery, walked around on the cemetery's hills, and snapped, with his pocket-sized digital camera, approximately three hundred images. He narrowed his choices down to sixteen, which served as the departure point for his drawings. Generally (although the artist considers them as mere source images), Gibbs's crisp black-and-white photographs reveal the notions of order, austerity, and eternity fostered by the cemetery's architecture and atmosphere. In one photograph, he captures an organically shaped cloud casting a shadow on a part of the lot, creating a tension with the evenly laid-out geometrical gravestones on a slow hill. In the photograph, one is able to see details of the inscriptions on many of the gravestones. Their function as monuments is both challenged and emphasized by the inclusion of a shadowed area, which implies the passing of time. As seen in the large drawing titled *Arlington* (p. 47, no. 4), Gibbs's translation of the source photograph to heavy paper removes density, high contrast, and specific details (such as the names of the deceased) found in the photograph. In his drawing, one can almost differentiate each grain of graphite, many of which constitute a depicted object. A closer look at the drawing reveals a matrix of marks that can be compared to a half-tone dot pattern. The resulting drawing is a pixelated image, an abstracted trace of the base photograph, unlike a realistic drawing produced through the use of the camera obscura. Gibbs's drawing is now several layers

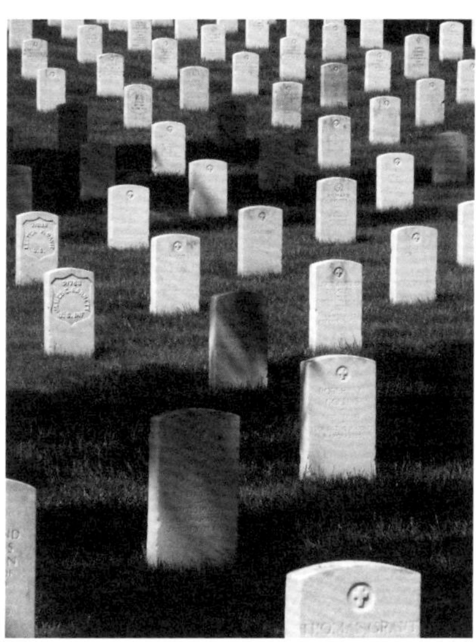

Ewan Gibbs, British, born 1973, Source
photograph for the Arlington series, 2010

removed from the source photograph, and the image appears to be evaporating or dissolving before our eyes. The image appears blurred, losing its site- and time-specificity, suspended between a photographic representation and memory. Although the drawing is abstract, even difficult to decipher, it nonetheless possesses the power to evoke the receding remembrances of loved ones who have died. We look at Gibbs's drawings with our eyes wide open, but the effect parallels the way images of people or places appear to our mind's eye when our eyes are closed. Arguably, Gibbs's process of translation/transformation can be compared to Roland Barthes's understanding of the act of looking away from a photograph or closing one's eyes "to see a photograph well."[2]

MEMORY, AND PHOTOGRAPHY, AND GIBBS'S DRAWINGS

Photography historian Geoffrey Batchen argues that a photograph can reflect only a frozen or still aspect of a memory, and "does not enhance memory—involuntary, physically embracing and immediate memory—but rather replaces it with images—images that are historical, coherent, informational."[3] He explains that a photograph can only "induce the full, sensorial experience of involuntary memory" and bring forth the present out of the past when it is "transformed."[4] Gibbs's digital source photograph reflects a systematic and detached approach to capturing or recording the loss of a fallen soldier. The camera coherently and evenly consolidates a collection of numerous individual deaths into a mere document. Because of his notational mark-making system, Gibbs puts his own imprint on the image of a gravestone, and revitalizes it. This is to say that Gibbs makes the gravestone anonymous by further abstracting the identity of the person buried at the cemetery. The now-abstracted image of the gravestone has transcended time and place, allowing it to function as a marker of both recent as well as more historically removed wars; the gravestone of a single soldier becomes the gravestone of all soldiers. Arguably, his active transformation of a photograph into a drawing liberates the image from being relegated to the realm of the forgotten or the static. The work, as translated, entices the viewer to return to the "involuntary, physically embracing and immediate memory" of those lost. Simultaneously, the drawing regains the "aura" of a work of art—to use a concept developed by Walter Benjamin—which was lost when a gravestone was made into a mechanically reproducible photograph.

Beginning in the mid-1830s, William Henry Fox Talbot desired to permanently freeze a latent image of a subject that interested him—a subject at a transitory moment, a subject disappearing or changing rapidly. Starting with a photogenic drawing process that he created in 1841, he soon invented a *calotype*, or paper negative process: a method of making paper negatives by chemical development to create a salted paper print.[5] Pursuing the interest in this technology, Talbot, one of the early inventors of photography, focused on a monumental column under construction, namely the Nelson Column in London's busy Trafalgar Square; and on a decaying abbey built in the twelfth century and located in a rural area in Scotland where the tomb of the well-known and popular author Sir Walter Scott is found. In the midst of a nation experiencing modernization, with flux and chaos in the air, in 1844 Talbot photographed the Nelson Column in Trafalgar Square (the square was completed in 1845). The newly developed public square with wider streets symbolized the dynamism of the city of London at that time. Instead of shooting the entire column from a distant vantage point, he chose to centrally frame the massive base of the column, a modern-day monument, surrounded by the steel frames for construction. One sees in the foreground the construction fence where posters are placed, and in the distant background the steeple of St. Martin-in-the-Fields; Talbot juxtaposes modern elements with the faraway church, and his focus on this juxtaposition almost suggests that the historical architecture is going out of fashion. Employing the just-invented process, Talbot's *Nelson Column* marks the intersection of the old and the new. At about the same time and perhaps with a splash of nostalgia, Talbot turned to another subject, a historical memorial, seeking to freeze and thereby memorialize the continuing deterioration/ruination of the twelfth-century Gothic-style abbey that had been burned twice. With the camera, Talbot attempted to intervene and momentarily halt the decaying of the abbey, as if he himself had the ability to "stop" time.

Despite the distinct quality of the Talbot prints from the MFAH photography collection (due to the museum's regulated preservation environments), inherently, they are unstable, and have been slowly fading in their color (from original dark chocolate brown), tonality, contrast, and losing details since their creation in the mid-1840s.[6] In a sense, then, gradually the images are becoming abstract, or, more aptly, they are dissolving and evaporating, and returning to their latent state, which makes an interesting comparison to Gibbs's approach to transforming his photographs into drawings. In theory, Talbot's photographs and Gibbs's drawings began at opposite ends of the spectrum (between a photograph and a graphite drawing), and now they are slowly bridging the gap. Talbot's photographs of two famous monuments, originally captured with light, are becoming static and ephemeral images by default; Gibbs's drawings of Arlington National Cemetery, which he transforms from his own, necessarily static photographic images of the gravestones, serve in real time to invoke quiet but powerful and involuntary memories of the deceased—a figure (or figures) made anonymous with the blurring of names and other details, rendering the gravestones ever-present memorials to *all* soldiers. The result is that the viewers of Gibbs's drawings can conceivably project any name onto the blurred or blank "screen" of the gravestone, even their own.

1. *The Tomb of Sir Walter Scott* is included in Talbot's second photographically illustrated book, titled *Sun Pictures in Scotland,* published in 1845. (His first photographically illustrated book was *Pencil of Nature* [1844].) With no text other than a list of plates, Talbot transported the reader via photography to sites significant to the life and writings of Sir Walter Scott (1771 – 1832), a popular British novelist, playwright, and poet. "William Henry Fox Talbot: The Tomb of Sir Walter Scott, in Dryburgh Abbey (1997.382.4)." In *Heilbrunn Timeline of Art History.* New York: The Metropolitan Museum of Art, 2000 – . http://www.metmuseum.org/toah/works-of-art/1997.382.4 (October 2006)

2. Roland Barthes, *Camera Lucida: Reflections on Photography,* trans. Richard Howard (New York, New York: Hill and Wang, 1981), 53.

3. Geoffrey Batchen, *Forget Me Not: Photography and Remembrance* (New York, New York: Princeton Architectural Press, 2004), 94.

4. Ibid.

5. Richard Benson, *The Printed Picture* (New York, New York: The Museum of Modern Art, 2008), 102.

6. This observation was made based on the author's discussion with Del Zogg, manager of the Works on Paper Study Center, and Toshiaki Koseki, the Carol Crow Conservator of Photography, respectively, at the Museum of Fine Arts, Houston. Specifically, regarding the fading of color of Talbot's print *The Tomb of Sir Walter Scott,* curator and photography historian Malcolm Daniel points out as follows: "[c]opies of this image in *Sun Pictures*…faded dramatically from their original dark chocolate brown even in Talbot's time, due to impurities in the Reading printing establishment's water supply, to the printer having inadequately washed out of the hypo fixer, and to the publishers having trimmed and affixed them to bristol, which left them more vulnerable to oxidation and exposed them to chemicals in the mounting glue." See Malcom Daniel, "Inventing a New Art: Early Photographs from the Rubel Collection in The Metropolitan Museum of Art," *The Metropolitan Museum of Art Bulletin,* vol. 56, no. 4 (Spring 1999).

All drawings are by Ewan Gibbs
British, born 1973.

1 *Arlington* [1st large], 2012
pencil on paper; sheet 45.5 cm × 30.5 cm;
image 36 cm × 27 cm; grid 2 mm × 2 mm.

2 *Arlington* [3rd large], 2012
pencil on paper; sheet 45.5 cm × 30.5 cm;
image 36 cm × 27.2 cm; grid 2 mm × 2 mm.

3 *Arlington* [6th large], 2012
pencil on paper; sheet 45.5 cm × 30.5 cm;
image 36 cm × 27 cm; grid 5 mm × 5 mm.

4 *Arlington* [2nd large], 2012
pencil on paper; sheet 45.5 cm × 30.5 cm;
image 36 cm × 27 cm; grid 2 mm × 2 mm.

5 *Arlington* [5th large], 2012
pencil on paper; sheet 45.5 cm × 30.5 cm;
image 36 cm × 27.2 cm; grid 4 mm × 4 mm.

6 *Arlington* [4th large], 2012
pencil on paper; sheet 45.5 cm × 30.5 cm;
image 36 cm × 27 cm; grid 3 mm × 3 mm.

7 *Arlington* [7th large], 2012
pencil on paper; sheet 45.5 cm × 30.5 cm;
image 36 cm × 27 cm; grid 3 mm × 3 mm.

8 *Arlington* [8th large], 2012
pencil on paper; sheet 45.5 cm × 30.5 cm;
image 36 cm × 27.2 cm; grid 4 mm × 4 mm.

9 *Arlington* [7th small], 2012
pencil on paper; sheet 30.5 cm × 23 cm;
image 12 cm × 7.9 cm; grid 1 mm × 1 mm.

10 *Arlington* [5th small], 2012
pencil on paper; sheet 30.5 cm × 23 cm;
image 12 cm × 8.2 cm; grid 2 mm × 2 mm.

11 *Arlington* [2nd small], 2012
pencil on paper; sheet 30.5 cm × 23 cm;
image 12 cm × 8.8 cm; grid 1.5 mm × 1 mm.

12 *Arlington* [6th small], 2012
pencil on paper; sheet 30.5 cm × 23 cm;
image 12 cm × 7.6 cm; grid 2 mm × 2 mm.

13 *Arlington* [1st small], 2011
pencil on paper; sheet 30.5 cm × 23 cm;
image 12 cm × 8.3 cm; grid 1 mm × 1 mm.

14 *Arlington* [8th small], 2012
pencil on paper; sheet 30.5 cm × 23 cm;
image 12 cm × 7.9 cm; grid 1 mm × 1 mm.

15 *Arlington* [3rd small], 2012
pencil on paper; sheet 30.5 cm × 23 cm;
image 12 cm × 8.1 cm; grid 1.5 mm × 1.5 mm.

16 *Arlington* [4th small], 2012
pencil on paper; sheet 30.5 cm × 23 cm;
image 12 cm × 8.8 cm; grid 2 mm × 2 mm.

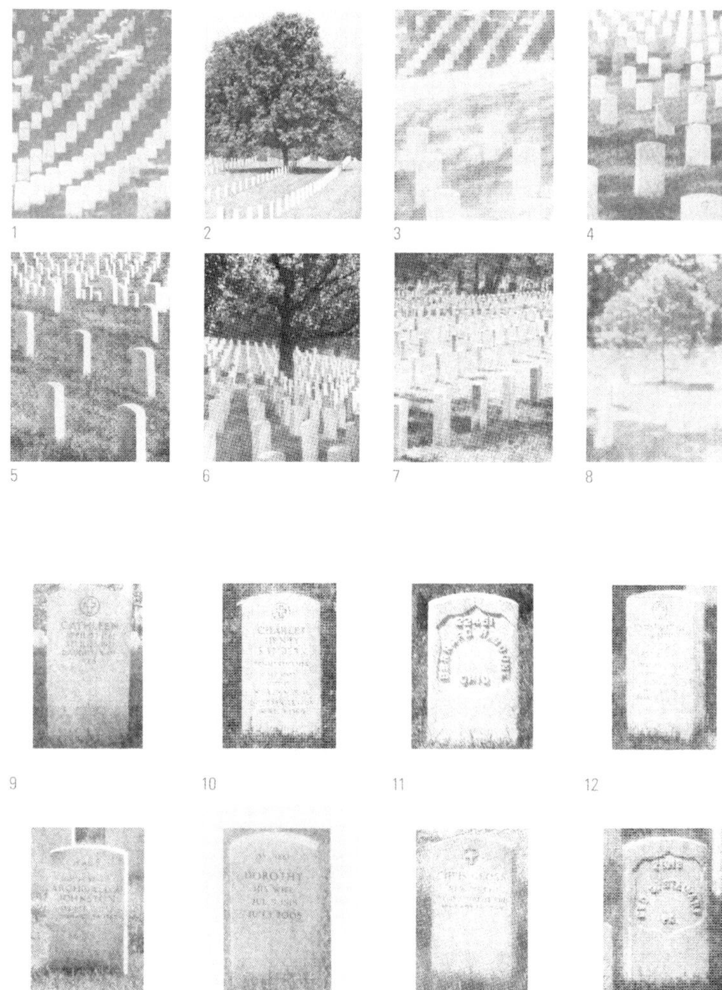

This book was published to accompany the exhibition *Ewan Gibbs: Arlington National Cemetery* that was organized by and presented at the Museum of Fine Arts, Houston, from November 11, 2012, to February 10, 2013.

Jacket & book design by Daphne Geismar

Typeset in Univers by Daphne Geismar

Printed by The Studley Press in the United States of America

Distributed by Yale University Press
New Haven and London
www.yalebooks.com/art

Library of Congress Cataloging-in-Publication Data:

Shiff, Richard.

Arlington National Cemetery: drawings by Ewan Gibbs / by Richard Shiff; with contributions by Ewan Gibbs, Rebecca Dunham, and Yasufumi Nakamori.

pages cm

Summary: "Ewan Gibbs (born 1973) has trained his expert eye on Arlington National Cemetery, the most hallowed resting place for many who gave their lives in service to the United States. Gibbs has created drawings of masses of graves and individual grave markers. Although the subject is recognizable, each image appears abstract, and some-how fleeting, upon close observation" —Provided by publisher.

Issued in connection with an exhibition held Nov. 11, 2012 – Feb 10, 2013, Museum of Fine Arts, Houston, Texas.

ISBN 978-0-300-18504-1 (pbk.)

1. Gibbs, Ewan, 1973– —Themes, motives. 2. Arlington National Cemetery (Arlington, Va.)–In art. I. Dunham, Rebecca, 1973– II. Nakamori, Yasufumi. III. Gibbs, Ewan, 1973– —Drawings. Selections. IV. Museum of Fine Arts, Houston. V. Title.

NC242.G465A4 2012I
741.942–dc23

2012034195